Ben Fagan is from Hawke's Bay, Aotearoa New Zealand. He discovered poetry in 2012 after attending an event by Poetry in Motion Wellington, where he was inspired by three performers (Ali Jacs, Duncan Hope and Luka Lesson) to sign up for the next open mic.

Two chapbooks, a USA and a NZ tour later, Ben travelled to the UK to perform his solo show *Under the Table* at the Edinburgh Fringe Festival 2015. The following year he returned with *Made to Measure*, a two-hander poetry show co-written with UK Slam Champion Sara Hirsch. In the same year, along with Sara, he won the Edinburgh Fringe Anti-Slam and came second in the national finals, making them the second-worst poets in the UK.

Ben is a producer and coordinator for New Zealand Poetry Slam, Poetry in Motion Wellington and Apples and Snakes. He splits his time between aeroplanes, stages and Pokémon battles.

www.benfagan.nz

facebook.com/benfaganpoet

Illustrations by David Prentice, who fought London and drew. He is also from Hawke's Bay and has the following advice:

'Travel is harder than MacBook blogs make it out to be, but there are truly beautiful moments to be experienced with absolutely nothing in your pocket. The world is still untamed, adventure still exists, monsters are still real.'

Instagram: @david_prentice_art

etsy.com/shop/DPartDesign

SOME TRAVELLER

Ben Fagan

Copyright © 2017 Ben Fagan
The author asserts the moral right under the Copyright, Designs and Patents Act 1988 to be identified as the author of this work.

All rights reserved. No part of this publication may be reproduced, stored in a retrieval system, or transmitted, in any form or by any means without the prior written consent of the author, nor be otherwise circulated in any form of binding or cover other than that in which it is published and without a similar condition being imposed on the subsequent purchaser.

This edition published by Bx3
an imprint of Burning Eye Books
2017

Burning Eye Books
15 West Hill, Portishead, BS20 6LG, United Kingdom

ISBN 978-1-911570-40-0

'Texts' first published in *Under the Table* (PiM Press, 2015).

Quotes from Oneika Raymond and Paula Varjack used with permission.

Edited by Harriet Evans, Tiho Mijatov and Sara Hirsch.

Author photo by Tyrone Lewis.

Cover design by Michael Gray.

For Nan

CONTENTS

BAGGAGE	14
SIXTEEN LITTLE THINGS I WISH I KNEW WHEN I GOT TO LONDON	15
UP IN SMOKE	16
THE HOLY TEE	18
VOLUME	20
HE TĀNGATA	24
FIREFLY	26
PRAYERS FOR THE NEW ZEALAND ACCENT	27
THE MUSIC OF THE NIGHT TUBE	29
PHRASEBOOK	31
FLIGHT 433	34
BACK AGAINST THE WALL	36
SHOULD I BRING ANYTHING?	37
GOOD MORNING	39
IN TRANSIT	40
CONTACTLESS	44
IN BRIEF	45
SEARCHING FOR STEPHEN	46
THE DAYTIME OF THE NIGHT	48
TEXTS	49
CRUMBLE	54
CHEESE AND CRACKERS	56
EULOGY FOR A LITTLE DOG, FROM THE OTHER SIDE OF THE WORLD	57
RADIO	59
REVIEWS	60
GREENER PASTEURS	66
DEFIANT or CHAINSAW ZOMBIES	67
IT'S A TEST	69
TIE DYE AND SOUTHERN TARTAN	70
PARTING THOUGHTS	71
GLOSSARY	75
RESOURCES	76
REFERENCES	78

SOME TRAVELLER

Whāia te iti kahurangi
ki te tūohu koe me he maunga teitei.

Seek the treasure you value most dearly; if you bow your head, let it be to a lofty mountain.

Whakataukī / Proverb

In William the Conqueror's time London was the size of Oamaru.

Owen Marshall (1992)

BAGGAGE

When I was born I weighed 3.9 kg, which is a good size for a carry-on.

SIXTEEN LITTLE THINGS I WISH I KNEW WHEN I GOT TO LONDON

1. If you order a pint and they go for the hand-pull, there's a good chance it's going to be flat and warm.
2. Trains are named after their final station.
3. Satsumas = mandarins
4. ANZAC Day remembrance is in Hyde Park Corner.
5. Cruskits = cracker bread
6. New Zealand Marmite ≠ British Marmite
7. If you're looking for Tim Tams, try Penguins; they're roughly the same and come with jokes.
8. Prosecco = sparkling wine
9. If you wear your jandals after it's been raining you'll have black toes when you get home.
10. 'Squeezable honey' ≠ honey
11. Tipping is a thing.
12. In an emergency call 999.
13. Postcodes are very important.
14. Squash ≠ a type of pumpkin
15. Londoners you know will loudly talk to you about the most personal things on packed trains because they know they'll never see these people again.
16. Saying 'we don't have this back home' isn't always true; often you just didn't know something.

UP IN SMOKE

Every colony knows the worst of its motherland.
From far away our families look back
at the island of coins,
the giant with friendly shoulders and dark past.

Kids sit at the back of the bus with 50c,
slowly scratching progress into the glass,
afraid of the cracks but scratching anyway.
We know the power of small change.

40°08'08.6"S 176°09'41.6"E

Building a fire is like climbing a mountain,
she told me, looking down in boots and blazer.
You gather the things you need,
then begin at the base.

Warmth comes slowly as you ascend.

Mountains are built in ink,
she taught me, they are sketched and planned.
With her finger she underlined
the skyline with a red zigzag.

A clay student is hopeful.
A brick student is insulted.
The only difference is heat
and planning.

By the end of the day she has built a bridge of me
and has enough left for a brazier on the other side.

Suddenly, always, the sun is setting
and we don't get a chance to write poetry.

Instead we sit side by side and
stack single lines like kindling,
fan the flames until we are

glowing outlines of ourselves.
She is the best of the city.

Barely noticing the paths are burning.

Finding the summit against all odds.

THE HOLY TEE

Every Sunday I go to Tesco.

Pass Peter the security guard. Pass miraculous fruit,
giant strawberries and mid-winter mangoes.
Pass enough discounted sandwiches to feed
five thousand.

I'm on a mission:

- Tea bags
- Mandarins
- Bread

Aisle two, shelf two. Check us today, our daily expiry.
I pass over the older loaves
even though the golden rule is baked into me.
Dough unto others…

Parishioners in the biscuit aisle bend over to collect their
morning sin. Patterned hoodies clutch one too many
items and mouth confessions of regret,
pride stops a trip back for a basket.

The final aisle is my favourite.

Bottles watch our shuffling procession
towards payment,
stretch their necks to see
what we're buying that morning.

They have the names of French martyrs:
Saint Sauvignon Blanc, Saint Pinot Gris.
They are messengers from the kingdoms of
Jacob's Creek, Villa Maria and *Tesco's Finest.*

My homesick eyes pore over their labels and locations.

'I've been there,' I tell no one.
'That's where I'm from.' No one cares.
Saint Sauvignon of Marlborough knows me.
We share a respectful nod before awkwardly looking away.
It's complicated. Let's just say she'd lose her halo
if it wasn't screwed on.

Opposite, behind the counter, spirits ascend
towards the ceiling and await our eventual arrival.
I cross the final threshold when I am beckoned
by the man with the prophet's name.

He takes my payment
and judges it worthy
with eyes preaching late nights
and early starts.

I thank him, then smile at Peter on my way out.
We are equals now.
Plus I didn't take a receipt
and don't want to be stopped.

Through the automatic doors
I step over a man with red and white eyes.

Avoiding his glassy stare
I carry my bags off down the road,
leaving one set of reusable 10p footprints
and a man hungry on the ground.

VOLUME

London is the same as anywhere else,
just with the volume turned up.

Hendrix played on this stage, poet.
Pink Floyd got their start right here.
That fountain you're admiring?
It hasn't changed since Dickens wrote about it.

Maybe, hypothetically,
despite an early bedtime
you'll suddenly have to call 999.
Maybe you'll find yourself ushering
two paramedics into your kitchen at 1AM.
One of them from 'the middle of nowhere'
near Melbourne.
When it takes two of you to stop the bleeding,
he'll cheerfully say, 'There, just like Gallipoli,'
and you'll laugh and feel better.

You know, hypothetically.

Ten-year-olds will scream memes at you.
Travellers will sit next to you in an empty carriage.

In London, you are the same as anywhere else,
just with the volume turned up.

There were queues to catch the train, queues even to obtain a soft drink. Everything's a queue. Once I went for a swim in the Serpentine and had to stand in a line about five chains long – to go for a swim!

Inia Te Wiata (1976)

There are two places in the world where men can most effectively disappear – the city of London and the South Seas.

Herman Melville (1859)

HE TĀNGATA

Rebecca is a runaway.
She hits London like a treadmill,
singlet printed with raised middle finger,
letting her cider know
to keep its distance.

She says changing countries is like junk food,
feels good but doesn't fix your problems.

Rebecca works for a gym,
has a million useless followers on Pinterest and
describes herself as a professional comparison maker.
First between here and there,
now between this and that.

        Sunlight glances off Rebecca's laptop,
           looking for an outlet.

                Johnnie is a man of the earth,
              he stands like a rock and watches
                  the multi-coloured flotsam
              washing in from Camden Lock.

        There was a fire in the market last week.

                The Japanese Cultural Store staff
                and the woman from Yumchaa
                  agree that his pounamu
                    saved the room.

        Sunlight reflects off the fire truck,
    reminds Johnnie of his daughter in Takapuna.

Tania takes a taxi from King's Cross,
takes the Overground to the glistening river,
takes the lift to the ground floor.

Tania takes a left, then a right,
then another left.

She tells me it's an accident,
that she followed the kōwhai
and found herself in a house
at the top of the mountain.

Makes a strong net from
the flax in the garden
and the rugged individuals
her priority.

                Sunlight reflects off a London bus,
                    catches Tania's eye.

                          Clint helps the people pull together,
                      raises money for the stabbing victims
                              and knows the cops.
                          Clint catches a Nelson swell,
                    surfs in to save the new swimmers
                            who have no idea.

Don was dressed as a zombie when he met his
new flatmates; they wouldn't let him in.
Charlotte's flat fell into a sinkhole.
Claudia asked for six and was misunderstood.

                              Clint has heard it all before.

      The runaways don't wait for others to catch up;
              the chase is half the fun.
            They hide online across London.
             Catch the sun where they can,
               and take it with them.

FIREFLY

The old woman stands still as guilt
with a familiar squint.
Firefly cigarette flying a slow circle
from waist to face and waist again.

We walk past her every night.
She avoids our eyes, in silent defiance.
Every night we nod
to our most loyal audience.

I wonder if she notices how
after each nightly trip we walk a little closer.
Each shared evening giving
another reason to brush shoulders.

Our staggered conversation
somehow finds its way down the dark street.
Curious fingers flying a slow circle
from phone to face to phone to waist.

Our jean pockets are full of bees, buzzing relentlessly.
Everyone's been stung, except for our friend the firefly,
in smoky nightie,
avoiding our eyes.

PRAYERS FOR THE NEW ZEALAND ACCENT

I

God Defend New Zealand
(to be read aloud in a kiwi accent)

Yeah, g'day, God,

Look, I thought in a city of ten million I might blend in, and I almost do. But something frustrating happens again and again. Whenever I greet anyone, on the phone, or at a café, or when I check in to a bed and breakfast, I apparently misrepresent myself. They always seem to think my name is Paul or Dave, when I'm very clearly saying 'Ben'.

It's not just now and then, it's a trend. I'll be sitting here on this park bench, mid-English adventure, then some joker comes along and messes with my zen mindset. Don't get me wrong, I've made friends with every Glenn, Jen and Sven that's come across my deck. Everyone I meet here is tremendous, but there's no point pretending it's not offensive! I'm not having a go, that's not what I meant, and I don't want to be condescending, but it's not high-tech, is it? I'm not trying to reinvent the wheel, just dispense some wisdom without sticking my neck out. Prevent anyone else expending unnecessary energy fending off the mockery of some dense gent.

I commend those who share my dilemma and have the common sense not to get defensive. I can't comprehend why my accent is so hard to process.

That's my two cents, anyway. If you can help, God, I'd appreciate it.

Cheers, or, uh,
Amin.

II

London Velo Café

Barista:	Are you from Australia?
Ben:	Nah, New Zealand.
Barista:	Cool, I loved Australia, I have all the best memories of Australia. This one time in Australia…

III

Clare Brady: Australian, in a good way

Clare:	Oh no, I've forgotten my work pants!
Colleague:	You have special pants for work?
Clare:	Yeah, well, I don't want to ruin my regular pants.

THE MUSIC OF THE NIGHT TUBE

Hello!	*The Book of Mormon*
Starlight Express	*Starlight Express*
Opening Up	*Waitress*
Why God Why?	*Miss Saigon*
All Of London Is Here Tonight	*Finding Neverland*
Where Will You Stand When The Flood Comes?	*Parade*
Look Down	*Les Misérables*
Hello, Young Lovers	*The King and I*
Sweet Transvestite	*Rocky Horror Picture Show*
American Idiot	*American Idiot*
Big, Blonde And Beautiful	*Hairspray*
Sit Down John!	*1776*
I Can't Get Next To You	*Motown: The Musical*
Revolting Children	*Matilda the Musical*
Moving Too Fast	*The Last Five Years*
We Both Reached For The Gun	*Chicago*
Anything Goes	*Anything Goes*
No One Mourns The Wicked	*Wicked*
I'm Gonna Sit Right Down And Write Myself A Letter	*Ain't Misbehavin'*
Sanctuary	*The Hunchback of Notre Dame*
It Won't Be Long Now	*In the Heights*
Light At The End Of The Tunnel	*Starlight Express*
Waterloo	*Mamma Mia!*

Opening Up (Finale)	*Waitress*
A Whole New World	*Aladdin*
I'm Gonna Wash That Man Right Outa My Hair	*South Pacific*
If I Were A Rich Man	*Fiddler on the Roof*
Next Time, I Wouldn't Go Back	*Closer than Ever*
And I Am Telling You I'm Not Going	*Dreamgirls*
Deep Beneath The City	*In Transit*

PHRASEBOOK

How do I turn notifications off?
Jak wyłączyć powiadomienia?

Why is your watch on the wrong hand?
Perché il tuo orologio é sul polso sbagliato?

I'm afraid of thunder.
Tengo miedo a los truenos.

I'm fine with toasties again for dinner.
Είμαι εντάξει με τοστάκια ξανά για βραδινό.

We met at a poetry slam.
Nous nous sommes rencontrés à un slam de poésie.

My country isn't on your map.
بلدي ليس على خريطتك

Should I give money to homeless people?
Trebam li ja dat pare beskućnicima?

Your biscuits are boring.
クッキーの見た目も味もつまらない

I was in a viral feminist music video.
jag var med i en feministisk musikvideo som gjorde internet-succé.

What's your star-sign?
你属于哪个星座

Do you think Twitter has radicalised the left?
Denkst du Twitter hat die Linke radikalisiert?

Can I read you a poem?
Māku tetahi kōrero tairitenga e panui ki a koe?

She'll be right.
चलता है।

Let's keep it all the way real: there are circumstances, many of a systemic socio-economic or political nature, that keep some people at home while others hopscotch the globe.

Oneika Raymond (2016)

FLIGHT 433

Good evening, ladies and gentlemen, this is your captain speaking.

Welcome aboard this flight number ▇ to ▇ this evening. My name is ▇▇▇ which was mostly a result of a big Irish Catholic family. You will have noticed there is some cloud outside, but what we're really keeping an eye on is the ▇ should still be able to enjoy the majority of the flight.

For those of you sitting between rows 14 and 19 we have tried every trick in the book, to be honest, to fix ▇▇ some residue.

Your cabin crew this evening is led by George ▇▇ ▇ has it under control most of the time, but don't ask for tomato juice. He is being assisted this evening by Julie and Paul, who will make themselves available should you require it.

There is a selection of inflight entertainment for your ▇ have to think about where the director was coming from ▇ always thought of age restrictions more as loose guidelines.

Please keep your seatbelts ▇ event of an unexpected landing ▇ ▇ start a family, never look back. Make sure to turn your electronic devices to ▇ big, wobbly ▇ especially in the lavatories.

We will be flying down the eastern side of the country, so those of you on the right-hand side of the plane ▇ bit of a monkey ▇

██████ *Papa can you hear me?* ██████

██████ some residue.

Once we get under way I'll be sure to update you with any further details, but until then sit back, relax ██████

██████ need more than luck.

BACK AGAINST THE WALL

Instagram: @ben.fagan

This is where I am
This is where I am
This is where I am

Unsaid: Look, no filter
Unsaid: I am other
Unsaid: Hello?

SHOULD I BRING ANYTHING?

After 'Ease up on the drink, Sam' by the Alcohol Advisory Council NZ.[1]

Are you coming next Saturday?
Oh, it's pretty casual, Sammy,
something for the barbie, couple of brews, just leave
your mates behind this time, eh?

Oh, you know, 'shouty Sam'.
*Letting everyone on the Tube know
that you just think
that Brits don't get it, you know?
Too square and unfriendly, not like us, you know?
Not like us.
Everyone likes us.
What's not to like?*

'Punchy Sam'.
*Victims of entitlement gather around the pub table,
Instagram-hungry and Snapchat-blind.
She, the teacher friend invited along,
spent the day striking matches
for East London students.
At twelve they roll their own CVs and fill their pockets with heat
because the power's out at home.
Define 'perfect job', she says.*

'Hit on everyone's missus Sam'.
*Another round, love!
I've been here for six months today, so I can say
with some authority
that the EU is more irrelevant than Tui Blond
in a Brixton
pop-up
craft beer bar.
Where's that accent from, love? Germany?
Fifteen years in London!*

---

[1] https://youtu.be/v2lrGOIHLpc

Don't worry, I voted for the both of us.
Want to come back to mine?
You might not be allowed to stay here.

And I think that's when 'almost got arrested Sam' turned up.
Europe, seen through the bottom of a pint glass,
offers life experience like a mouthful of froth.
Tick countries off like an Italian coastguard fishing for illegals.
Inflatable novelty tongues can be used to sleep on cheap
flights, and to keep your head above water.
Three thousand refugees pulled from the Mediterranean Sea
in a single day.

Sammy, Sammy, we're mates, right?
I'm telling you,
you've just got to sort your privilege out.

Voiceover:
However you do it,
remind passengers to check their
baggage before boarding.

GOOD MORNING

Good morning.
I *London* you.

How'd you sleep?

Underground, is that my sweat or yours?
Is that perfume? I smell oysters.
Are you cross with me? Are you royalty?

Sprawling like a monarchy,
I saw a butterfly
in that Sunday park.

Our language was salty, sandy-haired
and watching 747 gulls circling above.
Let's fall in, London.

I'm keen if you are? Smiles rise in the east,
stringing a bow with fairy lights.
What fresh hell is limescale?

You lined me up front and centre, read me like poetry,
with plenty of eye contact
and body language.

The South Seas can't build cities like you.
All the bricks in the world can't stand the shakes we
brace against. My four walls fell away, I turned to clay,
we stole fire and found post enlightenment.
Royal male, that's me.

Sweet dreams, London.
Wipe away the soot that highlights your arches,
arch your back for me.

Tonight we sleep like living statues.
Frozen, dedicated, determined to prove that
you *London* me too.

IN TRANSIT

> *After 'For the Fallen' by Laurence Binyon.*
> *For Alexis, Tom and Scott.*

Through the spotty windscreen the road ahead was long and curving,
uncertain,
exciting.

Jokes rolled around our feet like bottles
as music blew in through the vents.
It was a slow start but eventually
our momentum took over.

When the accelerator collapsed
we turned on the high beams
to bury the highway
in light.

My eyes still close when the camera flashes.

Fence posts pass the passenger window and I fall asleep.
Each freshly painted milestone sticks in my dreams
like hardened, faithful Blu Tack
holding up a faded photo.

Out an airplane window
the scenery changes so slowly
it barely feels like
you're moving.

A well-travelled pocket of inactive
Facebook pages is a better marker.
Profile pictures grow stale,
while we who are left grow older.

At midnight, I see your face
39,000 feet above the ocean.
You smile and tell me a secret:

there are parts of the valley
the sun only touches as it sets.

Never tell them you can't do a thing. Get stuck in and have a go. By the time they find out you've never done it before, you're doing it.

Barry Crump (1961)

Only when you know your whakapapa can the mana of your ancestors shine upon you.

Eruera Stirling (1980)

CONTACTLESS

Chinese tourists run squawking from the gentle waves
in Mission Bay. English tourists smoke,
glance at the sunbathers, somehow manage to look like
men in togs with no intention of going swimming.
I can't believe the moustache is back.

I paint a Polish father and son
between the swaying pōhutukawa.

Six days a week, I watch them clean from my Stratford flat.
They treat the cars with respect, make sure each one rolls
out of their small garage looking a million bucks.
Six days a week they smoke and gossip and vacuum and polish.
Their catcalls are cash only.

An old mannequin stands guard at their storefront.

Once a week they rearrange her clothes,
make sure plastic shoulders are covered
so people don't think she's giving it away for free.
Word on the street is that she used to be a tourist too.
Before Brexit and border control.

They stand with her sometimes, lick cigarettes and make
the pigeons feel unwelcome. Two sets of eyes watching
boxes of PFC chicken strut down the road.

The Mission Bay beach can be summed up
with peach ice cream and payWave.
A vintage wooden cash register tells my contactless card
unbelievable stories about 'loose change'.
Ancient history.

Is your passport gold, silver or bronze?
Chinese and English tourists drop cruiseliner cash on gelato;
their BMW backpacks keep an eye out for the pickpockets
who weren't allowed in.

I don't let my eyes linger. This is their neighbourhood;
I'm just a visitor.

IN BRIEF

There is no middle ground
in New Zealand English
for one's undergarments.

Undies is a child's term,
jocks have sporting overtones,
panties strike me as American,
pants are British, as are *knickers*,
a *thong* has a sort of mythical vibe,
boxers seem appropriately adult
but hardly ever accurate,
while *Y-fronts* I've only ever
heard of on the telly.
Similarly, *tighty-whiteys*.

So where does that leave me
at 2AM, trying to communicate
what I desperately need back
from under your grandparents' bed?

SEARCHING FOR STEPHEN

There's no way to tell
what kind of man Stephen Ward was.
He was born 200 years before Mum inherited his
surname in a Fielding hospital.

Stephen was a printer in Soho, at a time when being a
printer meant being watched.

King George kept a register, maintained by his staff,
noting who had access to such powerful technology.
A few hundred years earlier, the first mass-produced
book had gone to print. A Bible, of course.

'What's the agenda of these printers?'
the priests whispered to each other.
'Think what one of their modern books might do in
the wrong hands, in a child's hands!'

Stephen printed sheet music,
notes kept in line by rainbows stamped straight.
Whenever music turned the pages, though,
they arched across the paper and caught the light.

Soho's history was still to come.
The lines were ruled, waiting for love
to be hand-pressed against walls and cobblestones,
handwritten on streets paved in glitter.

I hope Stephen took pride in his work.

We tried to find him,
after work one day,
in an overgrown cemetery
with hidden graves and a handful of souls at rest.

The stone walls were all that remained upright,
print impossible to read,
tombs worn with age.

Stephen didn't want to come out and say hi.

The newer headstones resembled Stephen's sheet music;
there was the title of the piece,
a time signature,
and some even had lyrics,

engraved in a modern form of English
that I'm sure Stephen
would have thought
was a bit queer.

#PrideInLondon
July 2017

THE DAYTIME OF THE NIGHT

I always thought 'sleep-learning' was pseudoscience.
There is no way you can learn another language overnight,
I would say.

That was before I left the window open one night
and woke up speaking exhaust pipe.

I can now fluently scream all the foxes' best pickup lines,
sympathise with the complaining boiler,
mumble with the fridge,
laugh with thunderstorms,
and paint with all the colours of the wind.

I can sing Arabic songs with Polish choruses
but never quite remember the words,
dispense elderly wisdom in five African languages
and end relationships with a cockney accent.
In short, I am now multilingual.

When the night's lessons are complete,
it's time to sleep

until the baby downstairs
wakes the bird on the roof,
who thinks he is a car alarm.

TEXTS

By Mike Fagan

New message:
Hi Ben. Mum told me yesterday for the first time why you fell out with your mate, I'm sure you found anger you didn't know you had. That comes from me. What an a-hole he is. He's the biggest loser, not being able to trust him. Rains stopped, have a good week. Daddy.

New message:
Hi Ben, couple of points about trailers I'd like to share with you. Always put the safety chain on the car. Never try and lift the trailer with anything in it, it will stuff your back. My mate Brian's sore back started from a trailer mishap. Cheers, Dad.

New message:
Hi Ben, well done on finishing your long academic career. A good sense of achievement. Not everyone finishes with a degree. Again, well done. Daddy.

New message:
Hi Ben, Dad here. You need money mate. The bills will keep coming in from now. I've been there too, but I had cheap accommodation. Get on the dole, get something coming in. Then continue looking. It's a jungle out there until you are earning. Good luck. Dad.

New message:
If you are cold calling people and there's a front gate, what we do is shake the gate before we open it. Any dog present will head for the gate before you go inside. Stay alive. Hah.

New message:
Big fireworks display in wellington harbour tonight –
I'll do a small one here for my Daddy's birthday.

New message:
Hi Ben. In a small flat it's hard to locate the smoke alarm away from steam, cooking smoke etc. If you have a new battery in it, and it's still beeping off and on, it will be a faulty smoke alarm. I will send you one :D Still sunny here.

New message:
Hi Ben, Got 2 pigs yesterday. Funny how it took some effort to set the alarm for 4:30 that morning but it all came right. The pigs were rooting around below that log you were sitting on in that nice little clearing :D

New message:
Don't worry, all us workers miss daylight this time of year.

New message:
Hi Ben. Raining here too, for a whole week they reckon. Little birdy told me you are thinking of a change of career. Well done. If you are thinking of jumping try to have somewhere to jump to first. I jumped many times, but always had a cheap bed at Grandma's to stay. Drying day today. Hot and windy.

New message:
Hi Ben. Well done with the grind. It makes the freedom years so much sweeter when they come. I know, I've been to the mountain top. Weather's great for next week. Cheers, Dad.

In a life the nucleus stays the same, but with any luck the circumference moves out.

Seamus Heaney
(Clarke, 2015)

London is the home I am forever questioning.

Paula Varjack (2016)

CRUMBLE

Take two cups of sliced apples,

re-read that Facebook message,
try to smile at the Tesco staff.

Fly back at short notice if you can.

A quarter cup of water
from the Air China flight attendants.

**Pour one cup of flour
and a ½ teaspoon of baking powder.**

Try not to yawn when you greet your country,
she is only the backdrop this time.

Remember ½ a cup of brown sugar.

Shift as much firewood as you can to save Dad's back,
pack the wheelbarrow in the same way you fill your bag.
Lift with your legs, you definitely should have one of
those suitcases with wheels by now.

Throw the roguish traveller you always wanted to be
on the woodpile; he was always too organised to sleep
under the stars. Think about work emails.

Add 50g of butter.

Waterblast the bricks until you feel like you're helping.
There's no point trying to stop the mud.
Sit by the bed and make small talk.
You can see the hills from here.
Say goodbye under your breath, again.

**Cook apples and water until just tender,
then put in an oven dish.**

Decide that four is too many times to hear the same
story from Mum, tell her and regret it while sifting flour
and baking powder.
Add sugar and make jokes,
you'll be back on a plane soon.

Rub in butter.

Sit uncomfortably at the funeral,
be glad you're there.
Think about how the hills looked
out the hospital window.

Spread the mix over sliced apples.
Board the airplane with butter still under your fingernails,
decide to leave it there for the time being.

Crumble in the heat at Guangzhou Airport.
It will be early summer.

Bake for about 30 minutes at 190 degrees Celsius.

CHEESE AND CRACKERS

My parents are sitting in a cheap Parisian restaurant,
looking out the window at the Arc de Triomphe,
looking small, scruffy, chuffed to be there.
Dad won't touch the snails,
Mum's enjoying the wine.

We make a game of the woman sitting alone.
I reckon her husband left her.
Sara reckons he died.

We define her by the people not present,
and by her worn, red feather boa.

Dad changes the subject, tells one of the old stories.
How a man with his name climbed the walls of
Buckingham Palace, nicked some cheese and
chatted to the Queen in her bedroom
before the guards showed up.

I tell Mum that I remember
her crying when Princess Diana died,
in our first house,
by the fireplace where they burnt
the old red wooden toilet seat.
A simple stone arch where Dad proposed
and was triumphant.

We sit with shared surnames,
distantly related to half the British tourists
on Avenue de la Grande-Armée.

I suggest that we get a cheese and cracker plate for dessert,
and a smile climbs up Dad's face,
looking for trouble.

EULOGY FOR A LITTLE DOG,
FROM THE OTHER SIDE OF THE WORLD

The little dog moved to the orchard.
Poked her black nose up at the trees and sniffed.
Within a few days she had met pūkekos and hawks and
bossy chickens and angry goats and hundreds of birds.

The little dog chased the birds.
As little dogs do.
Never with any hope of catching them,
never knowing what she would do if she caught them,
just chasing. Playing.
Motivating them to fly.

When she wasn't outside she would stay in the house,
head resting on the windowsill while the birds flew back
and forth from their nests,
further each time,
wings spread more confidently,
flights more exciting,
over fields,
overseas.

The little dog waited patiently until they returned and it
was time again to chase, and run, and sniff, and bark.
She got presents at Christmas and pigs' ears to chew and
wide spaces to run in. She hunted rats and, rabbits and,
wild cats, and possums.

She came when she was called.

One sunny autumn morning,
the orchard called the little dog's name.
She perked up her ears, wagged her tail,
and trotted out between the trees.
The sun was as golden as her coat when she paused,
lowered her head to sniff the ground,
and went to her final rest.

When word got out that they wouldn't be chased any more, the birds came to roost between the feijoas, on the empty apple branches. One heard the news in a London spring, another beside Sri Lankan surf.

They gathered to remember the little dog that
had protected their nest,
head on windowsill,
bark in the night,
wee on the postie.

She had been there when apples
were falling into exam timetables,
tail wagging and tongue out.

She was there when growing up
meant stress and heartbreak,
with muddy feet, damp coat,
and unapologetic expression.

The birds sat in the trees,
singing songs of their friend,
the little dog.

RADIO

Alexander Graham Bell is well known
for inventing the telephone.
Frank Bell was a sheep farmer
up Shag Valley, East Otago.

On an amateur setup
(which his grandson still looks after),
Frank was the first in Aotearoa to make contact
with London by short-wave radio.

He pinged off some Morse code,
which was picked up by a bloke
named Cecil in North London.

A couple of years later, when Frank had to go
back to the sheep, his sister Brenda took over,
becoming NZ's first female radio operator.

Frank and Brenda Bell.

>   *'Greetings from NZ – signed Bell'*
>   18 October 1924, 6.20PM NZMT

Skype doesn't seem to be working this morning.
Someone has probably driven into the junction box
down the road again.
I vaguely remember hearing a screech at 3AM.

Mum's expecting my call,
sitting on the couch in Whakatu with her tablet.
Waiting for the bell to ring, to see the modern miracle
that is my 7AM bedhead.

These calls are so early, by the time I've woken up
we're saying goodbye and I can barely remember
what was said. Though I get the vague impression
it involved how my sister is getting on.

REVIEWS

Book reviews from a notebook Nan filled for her book club between 2009 and 2014, found while clearing out her house. By Maureen Ward and Ben Fagan.

We're all in a book club,
following each other's plots and
swapping reviews.

> *The Witness – Nora Roberts*
> Intriguing mystery – couldn't put it down. It had a swim in the bath + I had to buy a new book. Excellent.

Mistakenly picking up
predictable paperbacks
from time to time.

> *Stolen – Lesley Pearse*
> Very basic storyline – I had guessed end of story about 3rd way thru book. Definitely last time I read her. Poor.

We notice the most compelling
writers keep their
curiosity.

> *Sun at Midnight – Rosie Thomas*
> I really enjoyed it. They followed our trip to Chile, Punta Arenas + then Chile airfield in Antarctica. Excellent.

They travel with purpose around their
worldly and statued
backyards.

> Note: 2 cheap books, took to Egypt and ditched.
> Note: Book bought at Valencia Airport.

Every time we meet, our first priority
is the weekly progress we weren't
present for.

> *Red Lotus – Pai Kit Fai*
> I took on my South Island tour.
> No time to get into it. Made a bird of it
> when back.

We chat and chuckle at the mistakes
our heroes keep
making.

> *Gypsy – Lesley Pearse*
> Fair only – Don't read any more of hers.

Some twists are so unlikely
you would laugh out loud
if they weren't so cruel.

> *Sing You Home – Jodi Picoult*
> Didn't like. Went thru how to go about IVF, including
> husband's part!! Then they separated. Miscarriages etc.
> Fair.

We're meant to prepare summaries, but when
the deadline comes around you can always
copy the back of the book.

> *Laid Bare – Rachel Francis*
> Autobiography. Didn't finish.

You can always choose your interests.

> *Spring Collection – Judith Krantz*
> Got bored. Gave up.

You can always forgive yourself if you choose wrong.

> *The Promise – Lesley Pearse*
> Strung out – could guess next move.
> Only Fair. NO MORE Lesley Pearse.

We silently review our own stories
much more than
each other's.

> *Water for Elephants* – Sara Gruen
> Old man 93 in nursing care, tells what happens there
> (bit close to home for me).
> V Good.

Hoping our hero kept a sense of humour,
surrounded by good people,
at the end.

> *The Year We Seized the Day* – Elizabeth Best + Colin Bowles
> Great read. I was laughing out loud all by myself. Excellent.
>
> Note: Lent to Raewyn

She may still exist in undiminished vigour when some traveller from New Zealand shall, in the midst of a vast solitude, take his stand on a broken arch of London Bridge to sketch the ruins of St Paul's.

Thomas Macaulay (1840)

A perfect summer day; cool breeze, brilliant sky, rich vegetation.

Mark Twain
(Hawke's Bay, 2 December 1895)

GREENER PASTEURS

In 1994, I was a toddler in Haumoana,
learning lines with a recurring cast of adults.

One of the more intriguing players was the milkman,
Frank, who had a truck that mooed.
I never found out whether the milk delivery trucks came
with this feature, or whether he installed his own mooer.

The delivery ritual was very complicated.
Empty bottles and money were left in the letterbox, then
coloured cards were mounted on the fence to indicate
the type of milk required: blue, yellow, green or red.

We were only in the market for blue and yellow.

Frank wore a bucket hat,
worked at the BP station for a while
after he'd given up the milk game.
Lots of local children wrote stories about Frank.

In 2014, I worked for the government in Wellington
issuing birth, death and marriage certificates.
Sometimes I got to use a big red stamp.

The older the certificate, the more shocking the language.
On a trip through family history you would meet *bastards*,
half-castes, *spinsters*, and a whole dictionary of awful names
for mental illness.

Office wisdom was held in a filing system of old ladies
in green cardies. They all retired before
we could teach Windows XP the same skills.
Sometimes their grandchildren wrote them stories.

History overlaps like a messy in-tray,
like a pile of change,
like unexpected memories.

DEFIANT or CHAINSAW ZOMBIES

3

The most London thing I've ever seen
happened in Croydon.

I was walking just off the high street
when a woman and her crying toddler caught my eye.
She whipped the child up into the crook of her arm,
yanked the kid's pants off, grabbed both ankles and
aimed through a chain-link fence into an empty car park.

The little person peed for their life,
like a squirming Super Soaker.

She held my gaze with all the confidence of an armed
police officer cradling a rifle with a full bladder.
The intensity of her stare absolutely convinced me that I,
somehow,
was in the wrong.

Her stare was London.

2

Fear was one of my first jobs. For five summers,
I was a 'scare-actor' in a dark corn maze.
Five summers spent silently laughing as massive
boys pushed their tiny girlfriends ahead of them around corners,
then lost their jandals running when I popped out to say hello.

If someone broke down in tears and couldn't go any further,
we would lead them out of the maze, calling the code word
'broken'
to avoid further surprises.

Friends asked if I got scared when left alone. I told them I'd
never felt so calm, between swaying corn and reliable stars.
The maze was my home.
Every dirt trail was a corridor between family rooms,
mad clowns and chainsaw zombies.
I was unafraid.

1

London is a maze, and we are well aware of its tricks.
If a truck drives into a crowd of people, we stand defiant.
If the vulnerable parts of our community
are harassed, we must make sure they feel at home.
If our leaders are the harassers,
we pick up our children
and teach them to call 'broken'.

London is a maze,
and we are the mad clowns
living behind each corner.
The dirty trails are ours.

0

Ready or not,
here we come.

IT'S A TEST

After 'Electron Test Flight One' by Rocket Lab.

A few years after
I swung too high on the swings,
Hawke's Bay reaches space.

TIE DYE AND SOUTHERN TARTAN

Tonight, the Tube lines twist away like tie dye. Fear
divides the train, frets over minutes that make no
difference above ground. Lost time in tunnels is more
frightening than closing doors, more present than the
colourful seats stained with the heat
of ten million second-hand bodies. Most of
our fellow passengers are asleep. Eyelids bottle the
early hours, a thin barrier in defence of imagined sun.

Tonight, the roads thread headlights like golden
stripes. Streetlamps weave southern tartan while lads
confess their love to dead phones and
look forward to forgetful mornings. Girls
tread the cracks between the concrete and all
ignore the ill-fitting parts of the city. They must.

> *This is a Golden Shovel poem. When read down the page, the final word of each line constructs two sentences from 'Fear no more the heat o' the sun' by William Shakespeare.*

PARTING THOUGHTS

'Big city,' she says.

'Yeah,
big city,'

he agrees.

'Good though.'

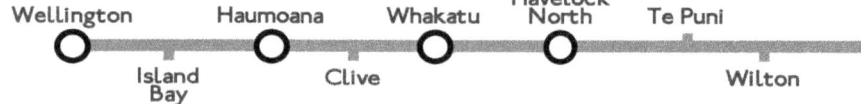

GLOSSARY

ANZAC Day	A national day of commemoration in Australia and New Zealand for those who have died in military service
Aotearoa	New Zealand
Haumoana	Small seaside town in Hawke's Bay
He tāngata	The people
Hīkoi	Journey
Jandals	Flip flops
Kōwhai	Tree with yellow flowers
Mana	Prestige or status (oversimplified, sorry)
Oamaru	The largest town in North Otago
PFC	London fast food restaurant, like KFC but worse
Pōhutukawa	New Zealand Christmas tree, often found on the coast at Christmas with big red flowers
Pounamu	New Zealand greenstone, or other treasure
Pūkeko	Purple swamp hen, seriously
Squiggles	Worth ten bourbon biscuits
Takapuna	A suburb on the north shore of Auckland
Tesco	British supermarket operating in twelve countries
Togs	Swimming costume
Tui Blond	A kiwi lager with a rating of one star on ratemybeer.com
Whakapapa	Genealogy
Whakatu	A NZ suburb best known for a freezing works that closed in 1986
Yumchaa	London tea store

RESOURCES

London

Kiwis in London
Getting young New Zealanders jobs, flats and drunk.
kiwisin.london
facebook.com/LondonKiwis
facebook.com/groups/KiwisInLondonChat

Runaway Kiwi
Blogging about coffee, culture and how to survive.
runawaykiwi.com

Hot News
My local for Squiggles.
facebook.com/hotnewsWIQ

New Zealand Cellar
The UK's leading NZ wine shop and bar.
thenewzealandcellar.co.uk

If the walls of the Tube feel like they're closing in, here's how to avoid the tunnels.
content.tfl.gov.uk/tube-map-with-tunnels.pdf

Also: Ngāti Rānana, Kea New Zealand, Hinemihi and the 'Southern Stand' War Memorial.

Global

Double the Quota
Raising New Zealand's refugee quota
doingourbit.co.nz

TransferWise
I genuinely recommend this as the cheapest way to send money overseas, plus, if you sign up with this link, you get one free international transfer, and I get some money. Thank you for your support. transferwise.com/i/benjaminf87

World Maps Without New Zealand
worldmapswithout.nz

I suppose, at some point, none of these links will work.

REFERENCES

Al Jazeera. (2017). Italian coastguard: 3,000 rescued in Mediterranean Sea. (Online). 7 May. Available at: www.aljazeera.com/news/2017/05/italian-coastguard-3000-rescued-mediterranean-sea-170507043116392.html (accessed Oct. 2017).

Binyon, L. (1914). For the Fallen. *The Times*, 21 Sept.

Clarke, J. (2015). Neva. *Mr John Clarke*. (Online). Available at: www.mrjohnclarke.com/tinkering/neva (accessed Oct. 2017).

Crump, B. (1961). *Hang On a Minute Mate*. Wellington: Reed.

Macaulay, T. (1840). On Ranke's History of the Popes. *The Edinburgh Review*.

Marshall, O. (1992). *Tomorrow We Save the Orphans*. Dunedin: John McIndoe.

Melville, H. (1987). *The Piazza Tales and Other Prose Pieces*, 1839–1860. Evanston: Northwestern University Press.

Raymond, O. (2016). Stop pretending everyone can travel. *Oneika the Traveller*. (Online). Available at: www.oneikathetraveller.com/stop-pretending-everyone-can-travel.html (accessed Oct. 2017).

Shakespeare, W. Fear no more the heat o' the sun. *Transport for London*. (Online). Available at: tfl.gov.uk/forms/12393.aspx?ID=112 (accessed Oct. 2017).

Stirling, E., and Anne Salmond. (1980). *Eruera: The Teachings of a Māori Elder*. Auckland: Penguin.

Te Wiata, B. (1976). *Most Happy Fella: A Biography of Inia Te Wiata*. Wellington: Reed.

Twain, M. (1897). *More Tramps Abroad*. Leipzig: Tauchnitz.

Varjack, P. (2016). Home. *Letters I Never Sent to You.* Portishead: Burning Eye.

Weir, J. (1998). *New Zealand Wit and Wisdom: Quotations with Attitude.* Auckland: Tandem.

Woodward Māori. (2015). *Māori Proverbs.* (Online). Available at: www.maori.cl/Proverbs.htm (accessed Oct. 2017).

ACKNOWLEDGEMENTS

Thanks to the multi-lingual treasures that are Bohdan Piasecki, Daniela Paolucci, Marcos Aaguilera, Nikos Gasialis, Amanda Green, Selwa Roberts, Tiho Mijatov, Tihana Mijatov, Sian Fleming, Agnes Török, Lee Ann Thevenet, Nadja Degen, Kimiora Paranihi, Te Kahu Rolleston and Alfred Lee.

Thanks to Jenn Hart and the Bx3/Burning Eye team for making this book possible, Sarah Fagan and Pim Greven for giving it an ending, Clint Heine for his endless support, Don McLeod, Charlotte Gardner and Claudia Taylor for sharing their stories, Rebecca Blandford for being bad at directions, Karen Fagan for the advice, Mike Fagan and Maureen Ward for contributing their poetry, Clare Brady for being the best antidote to pomposity, David Prentice for the extraordinary illustrations and friendship, Tania Bearsley for the tea, Travis Cottreau for everything, Anna Beecher for the recommendations, Neil, John, Simon and all the crew from Tina, We Salute You E20 for the flat whites, Tyrone Lewis for being so generous, Harry Baker for being so tall, Paula Varjack and Oneika Raymond for summing it up so perfectly, Fay Roberts for the quick turnaround, Blair Wotton for the three-year book loan, Mandy Klose for her urgent need to do good, Harriet Evans for catching them all, Jess Holly Bates for being the best dancer in any room, Michael Gray for being the whole package, NYDS for the help flying and Apples and Snakes for giving me a reason to get up in the morning.

Finally, the biggest thank you possible to Sara Hirsch, whose fire, compassion, talent and dedication to her work inspire me every day, and without whom I wouldn't have lasted five minutes in London. You've taught me so much more than how to pronounce Covent Garden.

אני הוא בתור.

www.ingramcontent.com/pod-product-compliance
Lightning Source LLC
LaVergne TN
LVHW041549070426
835507LV00011B/997